The Making Of High Achievers
(Trailblazers, Pathfinders and Trendsetters)

IKECHUKWU JOSEPH

Copyright © 2024 Ikechukwu Joseph

All rights reserved.

ISBN: 9798345963050

DEDICATION

to all aspiring high achievers

CONTENTS

1	Introduction	Pg.1
2	High Achiever/Achievement Defined	Pg 3
3	The Achiever and Mindset	Pg 5
4	An Achiever's Discipline and Habits	Pg 7
5	Achievers Inspirational and Motivational Quotes	Pg 8
6	Personal Growth Development	Pg 10
7	Critical Characteristic of High Achievers	Pg 12
8	High/Top Achievers Exemplified	Pg 13
9	The Making of A Champion	Pg 20
10	A Final Word	Pg 24

AppendixA:	Achievers Best Guide Series (BKS 1-5	Pg29
	About the Author	Pg31
	Author's Contact	Pg32

1 INTRODUCTION

- In life no one wants to or planned to be a failure. And no one was born a failure or a champion. Everyone want to be successful and a high achiever. None settles for an average but the way to achievement creates huge hurdles that we must overcome. This book is planned to teach you how.

- The journey to the promised land is a conceptual pursuit that involves a rigorous and purposeful process that will dovetailed into a successful productive end or achievement. So is the journey of achievement of achievers, top achievers, high achievers. This book, "The Making of High Achievers" is a concept of planned goal-oriented contents processed in a contextual milieu or environment. Achievers are not just born but are made. Champions, trailblazers, pathfinders, pacesetters or trendsetters didn't just happen but were created from scratch. It is a conceptual pursuit grown from progressive acquired content into an enviable height. During rough times or processes it is good to say, "don't give up, push - pray until something happens, tough times never last but tough people do, take one day at a time," but these pacifying words are not enough. You will be getting the wrong results if you continue doing the wrong things the same way. Let's learn from the examples of high achievers if we must join the train of trailblazers, pathfinders, trendsetters, pacesetters and top achievers. The making of high achievers. But what can we learn from such high achievers to make our life worth our while. The challenges these trailblazers listed below encountered and their successes are for our challenge:

— Elvis Aaron Presley: Best Musician of the Century
— William Shakespeare: World greatest dramatist
— John Stith Pemberton: Inventor of Coca Cola Formulae
— Pele (Edson Arantes Do Nascimento): Best Footballer of the century
— Booker T Washington: a slave turned American foremost black Educator

– Yamaha Torakusu: A cabinet-maker turned world largest manufacturer of musical instruments
– Phillip Emeagwali: Father of the Internet
– Elizabeth Blackwell: The first female doctor in the United States
– Apostle Joseph Babalola: Precursor of Pentecostalism in Nigeria and Founder of Christ Apostolic Church worldwide.
- If they overcame, you too can. If they traveled, you too can travel. Most of them started from nothing to something. More of their stories inside this book.

2 HIGH ACHIEVER/ACHIEVEMENT DEFINED

- Achievement definitively is often the output or outcome of a combination of inborn abilities and acquired developed skills. It is also defined variously subjects wise as the act of achieving or performing a successful accomplishment.
- A high achiever is a go-getter - an active and enterprising person; one who is motivated or inclined to excel; one who strives to achieve success or improvement. . A high achiever grabs challenges and problems with positive growth mindset, even in critical failure conditions adapt and turn things into gold. High achievers are the posibility advocates. All things are possible is their guiding principle or watchword. They continuously working hard, learning new things, trying new innovations in other to excel and come tops.
- A high achiever (HA) is someone who is successful in his life's career or endeavors by his efforts.
- Achievement goals according to Nicolas etal are based on these cardinal points:
  - Master a task and improve over time (Mastery Approach Goal),
  - Out perform others (Performance Approach Goal)
  - Don't fall short of mastering a task and never decline over time (Mastery Avoidance Goal),
  - Not be outperformed by others (Performance Avoidance goals).
- A high achiever's phobia in a poject is not failure but not trying or opportunity not to participate. High performers go for immediate gain but high achievers who are also high performer go for overall success. Someone can have high IQ without ending successful. A high-achieving child or workers who are potential high achievers need relevant push like praise reward, liberty to make choice, relevant exposure, experimenting with failure, practical, pragmatic activities and creative learning opportunities. They are competitive, natural but may not be great leaders, ambitious, great thinkers,

exploratory, hungry for success, determined, single-minded, focused and disciplined.

3 AN ACHIEVER AND MINDSET

- Mindset is defined as a way of thinking; an attitude or opinion, especially a habitual one. A mental system, set of beliefs of distinctive structures and processes.
- For a high achiever perfects his or her primary principles. A high achiever (HA) builds and rebuilds his foundational goals. Improving and perfecting something that has worked well for him. Kobe Bean Bryant an American professional basketball player often cited as one of the most dangerous scorers in the NBA was said to practice his lay-ups and his free throws daily before sunrise. Continuity in perfecting what you know how to do best is a good start in the right direction.
- HA embraces and recreates failure. High achievers mindset is that failure is not fatal nor that you are finished but the result of unfinished product waiting to be reproduced, reprocessed and polished. Failure is that you have learned your omissions, mistakes or what you did not do right or well at the last attempt. You can transform failure into a fortune by dealing with what went wrong. Failure is only a product of uncorrected mistakes. You must not major on your minors or minor on your majors. Keep the majors first and foremost. Your failure today must not terminate your future. Learn to forgive yourself your past mistakes.
- HA mindset is that you must not be limited by small success but be propelled by the unlimited God. Don't underestimate yourself. Don't focus on your inadequacies but manage them and your weaknesses for maximal output. Focus on your abilities and strengths. Strongly doubt your nagging pestering doubts. Even in failure, see failure as a way forward. Not that you have failed but that you have learned something from what went wrong in your first project or attempts.
- Surround yourself with the right kind of people and the wrong people with negative vibes will go. People who believe in you and your vision.

Positive thinking people with positive ideas.

- Setting Realistic Goals.

Set goals and objectives that are achievable within your capacity and available resources. Such goals must match your current skills, incentives, and time. This will help maximize resources available to you. Realistic achieveable goals helps you go from smaller objectives to bigger ones. From one success to another in a graded form. A realistic goal is one that's achievable and manageable within your current circumstances. For instance you can say, I will Learn to play all musical instruments in six months (unrealistic). I will learn to play rythmn guitar only in six months. The second option is realistic.

- Find your purpose and passion and pursue it vigorously.

"What are you good at? What do you enjoy? What are you good at that you don't enjoy? What are you not good at?"

Asking probing questions will help you identify your purpose and what you were created for.

-- Growth Mindset versus Fixed Mindset:

Mindset refers to the established set of attitudes held by someone, which can be broadly categorized into two types: fixed and growth mindsets

- Achievers with growth mindset embrace challenges seeing it as a way of improvement, going forward while fixed mindset avoid challenges maybe seeing it as interference.

- Growth mindset receive constructive criticism as useful feedback unlike fixed mindset

- Fixed mindset see talents as something static, stable and does not change. Growth mindset makes room for improvement in the abilities or skills.

- Fixed mindset focuses on the persons involved but growth mindset invest more on the process and not the end product.

- A fixed mindset sees their competition as a threat to their success and therefore treat them as such. On the other hand growth mentality learn and embrace the success of their competition and are inspired to progress.

- A rigid fixed mentality says no failure or mistakes but a company with growth mindset sees failure as an asset. You can learn from your mistakes.

- An operation based on a fixed mindset is afraid of introducing new innovation. Growth mindset go all out to look for something new, something better. They explore their environment.

- Our belief system determines how we react to changes, innovations, failures theories, hypothesis and life endeavors. People who believe all things are possible or they can do it have a growth mentality while others believe that their abilities are innate, already-made, follow come so to say and are limited to their capacity. No much change.

- those with growth mindset are high performers and hence are likely to end up as high or top achievers in their pursuit in life.

4 AN ACHIEVER'S DISCIPLINE AND HABITS

- Habits - an action performed on a regular basis must be the addiction of an effective high achiever. To keep development ongoing a positive habit of the production process must be cultivated.
- Procrastination they say is a lazy man's apology and is not for top achievers. They must build structures to possibly eliminate and overcome delays or unnecessary ungodly delays.
- We must differentiate high achievers from high performers. High achievers are characteristic of being their best in everything they do. They are perfectionists, always busy, enjoy their achievements and value their fulfillments in life.

5 ACHIEVERS INSPIRATIONAL AND MOTIVATIONAL QUOTES

- Words are powerful, creative and even lucrative. They say words have longer life than deeds. Hardly had words failed anyone except when not well processed or with an immature user. Shakers and movers of nations, pathfinders, orators, world leaders, successful politicians, great leaders have used the power of oratory, words of wisdom to change, rule, control, transform people's emotions, inspire their soul, motivate their contextual milieu, coerce them to join their cause and even manipulate them. Through mere but powerful words destinies have been shaped, nations created, hope restored and even wars and its vestiges adversely demonstrated. So are the wealth of words of wisdom in this book that will transform your life, sooth your soul, and even heal your body. Go ahead, and draw inspirations, strength, wisdom and motivations from these inspirational and motivational quotes. It is a life and game changer.
*****
- Meeting people make them relevant to yourself. The Moses that will bring you out of oddity, oblivion and the Joshua to follow up.
- It is not all about what you can get but all about what you can give.
- In spiritual warfare God want us to fight because He called us soldiers of the cross.
- Ill equipped leaders produces ill equipped people.
- Joseph went from kidnap experience to pit experience, to slavery experience, to prison experience to climb to the throne.
- Those who never face oppositions always stop at propositions.
- Lift up your eyes and look on the fields for there are viable opportunities.
- When you have concepts (revelation) the way you live changes

THE MAKING OF HIGH ACHIEVERS

- There is no victory without a war, no prize without a price and no crown without a cross.
- In discovery therapy you ask life's questions and uncover the problems so you can recover the solution.

*****

- Stop blaming God for your decisions.
- With God you can turn your impeaching importunities into optimal opportunities and frightful frustration into fortifying fortunes.
- You can turn your humble attitudes into higher altitudes.
- You can turn your distress disabilities into viable abilities
- Spiritual giants are only willing, available and thirsty spiritual babies who paid the price for the prize, who waged a war for victims to become victors
- You are not better than your thought. As a man thinks so is he.
- You do not need to be perfect to be the best.
- Old age is not a limitation or that your time have expired.
- Retirement is not that you are tired but that you have more experience.
- The cemetery is the richest or wealthiest prison of undiscovered, untapped, undeveloped and unfulfilled dreams.

*****

- You can create sense out of nonsense, something out of nothing.
- You can create wealth out of dearth, viable ventures out of turbulent adventures.
- You can create mercies out of miseries.
- You can create tomorrow's peace out of today's crisis.
- All the wicked are antagonist but not all the antagonist wicked.
- Every problem has one immediate cause, many remote causes, long term and short-term effect
- The difference between the ordinary and extraordinary is the extra. Go the extra mile and enter your extra ordinary success,
- You are the image of God so manifest his greatness in you.
- As long as you burn like oil you'll shine like light.
- God is a perfect matchmaker. Match your potentials with the right resources and manpower to explore and exploit it.
- Matching your potentials with the right credentials will crown your endeavors.
- Your identity or potentials need to develop relevance, get education, possess content and associate context

(for more see my book, 600 Life Transforming Quotes)

6 PERSONAL GROWTH DEVELOMENT

- Personal growth, self-growth, personal development so-called is a process of acquiring new skills, attitudes, actions, or reactions that can improve your life processes
- Personal development concept varies and can be classified into: mental, social, spiritual, physical and even emotional developments.
- Personal growth dwell or focuses on self-assurance, character, frame, and confidence. Practicing or working on such lifestyle improves your relationship with others. Creating and working on personal development goals help you discover where your strengths and weaknesses are thereby making room for improvements in life.
- Helping employees set unique and highly personal goals shows you value them and their contributions to the workforce. Appreciation of the admin encourage the young and upcoming employees.
- Outside organizational set goal, individuals can be encouraged to set their own goal for personal assessment in as much as it enhances their performance in the work place. Individual goals like having a cordial relationship with other workers and management, avoiding negative work ethics, speaking up useful suggestions for projects etc.

"Achieving success is not the key to happiness. Happiness is the key to success. If you love what you are doing, you will be successful." - Albert Schweitzer.

- High-achievers and high-performers are both consistently setting and reaching their goals. They are employers desire. While High-achievers are wired and driven by broad external inclinations high-performers are driven by immediate gains.
- If you will develop into high achiever you must develop a growth/innovative mindset. It might not be easy discarding your old retrogressive archaic mentality. You must embrace change, explore new

innovations as you work hard progressively in the right direction. Some work hard in the wrong direction. Better still in this age of technology work smart. Train yourself, your mentality, your innate concept, your acquired content, and even your environmental milieu and social settings.

- Both mindsets have their pros and cons. We must set up a control valve or monitoring device to know when to go or stop. You can also wisely apply an eclectic approach where you can use a combined effect in your operations where necessary.

7 CRITICAL CHARACTERISTIC OF HIGH ACHIEVERS (HA)

- HA must be optimistic and pragmatic. A practical person who make decisions and actions that are useful. Not just a theorist.
- They must be visionary persons. Someone having vision or foresight, revelatory ideals.
- Failures and weaknesses are seen as assets that can be explored and exploited.
- One's mindset whether positive or negative determines or influences one's personal and professional success.
- High achievers are goal-oriented hence they define achievable objectives and follow such to the later with zeal and zest.
- High Achievers are anticipatory, forward-looking and initiate proactive processes They act in advance to deal with an expected change, problems or difficulties in their workforce.
- They are flexible, strong and quick to return to the normal in the face of project accidents, damages, or shortfalls. Achievers are well motivated.
- Self-Discipline is their maxim, mantra, motto as part of their heraldic achievement. They are focused on the principles to reach their goals.
- Between the concept of each project's process and product they are effective managers of time and resources. Profitability and achievement are their active push-button. Effective time management is a critical skill for them to maximize creativity and meet their ultimate goal sufficiently.
- Motivation: HA are highly motivated personals by share aspirations, inspirations of their future and bigger set-goals.

8 HIGH OR TOP ACHIEVERS EXEMPLIFIED

Trailblazer/Achievers and Your Potentials (culled from my book, Discovering Yourself)

- The cemetery is the richest or wealthiest prison of undiscovered, untapped, undeveloped and unfulfilled dreams of presidents that never presided, great orators that never made a speech, astronauts that never went to the moon, doctors that never touched the sick or great preachers that never preached a Sermon

Trailblazers - their successes is your Chance, their rough path to the top your Challenge and their humble backgrounds your Change

Teach us to number our days and recognize how few they are; help us to spend them as we should (TLB) Ps.90: 12

Are you an achiever or under achiever, early achiever or late achiever? The idea of this chapter is for you to see the paths that these achievers traded to climb to the top. The interplay among forces of failure, struggling, suffering, hard work, courage, humble background, poverty, solutions and success in their endeavors.

Psalm 90:12 enjoins us to access and evaluate our time here on earth. Amplified Bible says, for. to number our days that we may get us a heart of wisdom. Ps 39:4 says let me know and realize how frail I am (how transient is my stay here). Friends, we must act now for our redemption is nearer than when we believed. We must give account of Gods deposit (our potentials) and time available to us. Dig for diamond and Gold. You were created for a purpose. Dont waste away.

Stay with your dreams, for these trail blazers did and history is telling their stories in golden, glossy and embossed shining foils.

CASE STUDIES OF SOME ACHIEVERS OR TRAIL BLAZERS OF OUR TIME

The idea here is to look at their success, poor background shortcomings and difficulties they encountered to the top, what challenges this will throw to maximizing our potentials.

REFERENCES: Information in this section came from -
-Encyclopedia Britannica 2002 Deluxe
- Microsoft Encarta
-Internet searches
- Literatures review, newspapers and other readings.

(1) NAME: Elvis Aaron Presley   The best musicians of the century (Guinness Book of Records) a former Truck Driver   Highest moneymaking celebrity even in death: 27 years after his death (2004), his records sold $45 million dollars.

BACKGROUND: Elvis (Norwegian name Alviss meaning All wise) was formerly a truck driver. Born in the humblest of circumstances in a two-room house in Tupelo, Mississippi, Jan. 8, 1935 to Veron and Gladys Presley. His twin brother was stillborn leaving Elvis as an only child who grew up dirty poor.

Elvis musical influences came from his parents Pentecostal church, gospel hymns, radio, pop, country music, all night gospel singspirations, and the-group sings at Rev. H. B. Brewsters black Memphis church. By this time he was not a composer.

In 1954 he began his singing career with the legendary SUN Records label in Memphis. By 1956, he became an international sensation. He broke social and racial barriers of his time and ushered in a new era of American music and popular culture. He dominated the Best Seller Chart (1956 58) and ushered in the age of rock and roll. Teen idol of the decade, greatest fans were white female working classes who passed Elvis ways to their children.

-He starred in 33 successful films.

-Sold over one billion records globally more than any other artist,

-Earned gold, platinum or multi-platinum awards for 140 different albums,

-14 Grammy nomination (3 wins) from National Academy of Recording Arts & Sciences, the Grammy lifetime achievement Award at 36,

-Named one of the ten outstanding young men of the Nation for 1970 by the United States Jaycee.

-He served his country also in U.S. Army.

-Died of heart attack at 42 in 1977 at is Memphis home Graceland.20 years later his Graceland became tourist attraction his records and other artifacts continue to sell robustly.

-Even in death Elvis still reigns in the record scene. A former truck driver?. What a challenge?

Stay with your dreams, for these trail blazers did and history is telling their stories in golden, glossy and embossed shining foils.

(2) NAME: William Shakespeare   He is regarded as the world greatest of all dramatists most famous writer in the history of English literature English

poet, actor and dramatist.

BACKGROUND: Shakespeare was an apprentice to a butcher because of his fathers financial difficulties i.e. He was learning how to sell meat. His education consists of Latin studies learning to read, write and speak the language and studying of some classical historians, moralist and poet. Shakespeare did not attain a university. He was born in a small grim-looking house of bricks in 1564, April 26.

PLAYS OF SHAKESPEARE (Out of 35 popular plays).

Plays: Julius Caesar, Macbeth, As You Like It, Hamlet, Henry Series, The Merchant of Venice, A Midsummer Nights Dream, Much Ado About Nothing, Romeo and Juliet, The Tempest, Twelfth Night, The Winter Tale etc.

For this poet, actor, dramatist who died April 23, 1616, his work is still relevant in our schools and educational systems after about 389 years.

HIS DIFFICULTIES: The disparity between the greatness of his great achievement and his humble origin of inadequate education and obscurity of life created doubts as to his authorship of such literary work. His writings reflected diverse disciplines like law, politics, linguistics, literature, history and geography, which were thought to be of one with vast background, which Shakespeare, has not. In fact, it seems evil people destroyed most of his manuscript to hide his identify as they are not preserved. He suffered great criticism and though dead his works (transformed potentials) lives.

INFLUENCE: His works are acted, shot as films, dramatized, or used as education literature.

CHALLENGE: Your writing potentials (still ideas inside you)? Your writing abilities (have written unpublished work)? Your writing prowess (enjoy rich writing culture)? Continue writing and look unto the God of providence. Your dreams can become reality.

Dont only preach the word but publish the word also. What you preach may disappear with time but what you publish will appear bigger, longer and may live forever. Doubt me? Check out Paul versus Apollos, the two great orators. Apollos varnished as his preaching was unpublished but Paul remains with the publishing of the Paulian Epistles.

(3) NAME: John Stith Pemberton (Invented formulae of Coca-Cola drink at age 50). Productive even in old age. Age was no barrier.

BACKGROUND: John, a man of great obsession, wanted to invent ultimate medicine and a perfect drink. He owned a chemist store and read about the virtues of coca plant as stimulant, aiding digestion, aphrodisiac and life extender. After much laboratory late night works and research, he combined cola plant and kola nut. Hence the compound name Coca-Cola. His early product was French wine coca but when in 1886 Atlanta city introduced prohibition of wine he substituted the wine in his drink with sugar syrup. His product plus advert marketing (introduced by his late partner, Frank Robinson) sold Coca-Cola today to become a multi-million dollar business. Though sick and old, Pemberton continued his research. He wanted something new, despite his breakthrough with Coca-cola. He later sold out the Coca-Cola formulae. John attended local school, later studied medicine and pharmacy at Reform Medical College, Georgia and Licensed to practice at age of 19.

CHALLENGES: Even in old age he was productive. He started as research to a heroic project. Like most inventors who rarely profited from their discoveries, John, because of lack of business sense lost ownership right, leaving his wife to die a pauper, though with a drink that came to represent the essence of American Culture. Pemberton died, August 16, 1888. his obituary described him as the oldest druggist of Atlanta. More than 125 yrs. later his laboratory is operative as part of Georgia Dept. of Agriculture. Today also the Bottling companies introduced the other products of the Coca-Cola Company like Sprite and Fanta and the world are enjoying the endeavour of this man called Dr John Stith Pemberton.

THE BIG QUESTION: Will old age or ill health or even lack of good education be a barrier to your developing your potentials? You only have the answer.

Dont only preach the word but publish the word also. What you preach may disappear with time but what you publish will appear bigger, longer and may live forever. Doubt me? Check out Paul and Apollos, the two great orators. Apollos varnished as his preaching was unpublished but Paul remained with the publishing of the Paulian Epistles.

(4) NAME: Pele (Edson Arantes do Nascimento) Best footballer of the Century (Guinness book of records). In this time he is still the most famous and best-paid athlete in the world.

BACKGROUND: He was born in an impoverished village of Tre Coracoes (Brazil) in 1940. His father was an undistinguished footballer who earned little. His mother was a cook who never wanted Pele to play football because of his fathers low income as a footballer. Pele at 15 watched hours as his father played. So Pele was so improvised as to use coconut as ball and tin cans as goal post. He suffered rejection from many league teams after playing for Sao Paulo state

His success: Played his first world cup game at 17,
-First player to play in 3 consecutive world cup finals
-Veteran of 4 world cup-scorer of 1, 283 first class goals.
-1962, best Player in the world.
-1978, recipient of the international peace award
-1980, announced the athlete of the century
-1973,South American player of the year
-1969, (Nov 20, in his 909th 1st class matches) scored his 1000th goal
-Published many best-selling autobiographies.
-Starred in many successful films
-Composed numerous musical pieces including the whole sound track of

THE MAKING OF HIGH ACHIEVERS

film PELE (1978)
-Pele Coca cola ranked as most popular brand in Europe.
I was born for soccer, just as Beethoven was born for music Pele.
CHALLENGE: What are you born for? The million-dollar question.
What you see only creates VISION. See problem from the eye of faith and not from the eye of fate or failure. See problem as a faithbuilder and not a fearbuilder. You must see problem as a hurdle to cross, an obstacle to dismantle, a mountain to mount on unto success, a sea to sail you through to the glory land. See problem as normal and not abnormal

(5) NAME: Booker T. Washington (a slaved turned American foremost Black educator of early 20th century).

BACKGROUND: Booker was a slave, denied early education. Born in a very small sized farm which he always call a plantation. His mother was a cook. He went to school not as a student, but to carry books for another mans daughter. It was illegal to educate slaves. After the emancipation proclamation in 1865, Booker took a job at salt mine that began at 4:00am so that he could go to school later. Later he became a houseboy to a wealthy town woman and at 16 he walked much of 500 miles to Virginia to enroll in a school for black students. BT overcame near impossible odds and helped black Americans uplift themselves and rose up from the economic slavery that held them long after their freedom from slave masters.

CHALLENGE: A slave overcame servitude and slavery but you are free born or are you in self-imposed slavery? You can excel better where a born slave did.

(6) NAME: Yamaha Torakusu a cabinet maker, founded the now world largest manufacturer of a full line of musical instruments Yamaha and leading producer of audio/visual products, home, sports, industrial and computer related products.

BACKGROUND: Torakusu a cabinetmaker was asked by a local school to help repair a reed organ from this he learned and built his own firsts reed organ in 1887 and later in 1897 formed Nippon Gakki Co. Ltd. (Japan Music Instrument) that later became Yamaha Company. Within the first year gained international reputation shipped 78 organs to south Asia. Then opened Furniture Company in 1903. Won grand prize at St Louis World fair in 1904 and died in 1917.

NOTE: From cabinet making to a world image-maker. Torakusu, the Man behind the success story of Yamaha Musical Instruments, Yamaha Motors, Yamaha Motor Cycle, Kawasaki etc.

7. NAME: Philip Emegwali Father of the internet.

BACKGROUND: Emegwali P. was born August 23, 1954 in Onitsha, Nigeria. Though very intelligent, he dropped out of school because of poor background of parents who couldnt afford enough money to train all their children. Philip however studied on his own. He was nicknamed Calculus as he mastered the subject at 14 and even out calculated his tutors. He sat for and got GCE from University of London and at 17 got scholarship to Oregon State University where he studied mathematics. After graduation he studied and got two masters degrees-one in Civil Engineering and the other in Marine Engineering. He also has a masters degree of University of Many Land and a doctorate (University of Michigan) in civil Engineering (scientific Computing).

ACHIEVEMENTS: Inspired by an article on forecasting of weather using 64,000 mathematicians, Emegwali designed a theoretical scheme for using far-flung processors that will distribute evenly over the world.

He worked on the connection machine, using 65,000 computers in parallel to formed the fastest computer in the world. It can calculate 3.1 billion calculations per second. This earned him the Gordon Bell Prize of 1989.

-1993 he got the Computer Scientist of the Year Award of the National Technical Association.

-1998- Distinguished scientific award of the World Bank.

-2001 - Best Scientist African Award of the African Broadcasting, heritage and Achievement Award

-2001 Gallery of prominent refugees of the U.N

-Emegwali was voted Historys 35th Greatest African in London (survey by new African magazine).

-1994 The Nigerian Achievement Award

-Profiled in the Book, Making it in America as one of the 400 models of Eminent Americans. Etc.

THE CHALLENGE FOR YOU: Lack of money did not stop his dreams. He used what he had his brains, to get what he wanted. You can create advantage out of disadvantage. What do you have? Nothing? No, you have life. You have a think tank or bank called brain. You have God. You have concept of who you are and what you were designed to achieve deposited in you at birth by God. You have a contextual setting (the people and the environment around you to exploit) and a content of experiential and acquired knowledge you have lived all your life. Do something now. I challenge you in Jesus name to be fruitful, productive and profitable.

Limitations have limits and expiring dates. Dont allow them limit or retard your life and potentials. Cash in on this

(8) NAME: ELIZABETH BLACKWELL - The first female doctor in the United States

BACKGROUND: Born: Feb.3, 1821 in Bristol England and died May 31 1910 at Hasting, England

ACHIEVEMENTS:

-Got Doctor of medicine in 1849

-In 1853 with her sister Emily founded New York infirmary for indigent women and children

-In 1864 organized US sanitary Aid commission

-Helped to found National health society of London and London school of medicine for women ETC.

THE CHALLENGE: During her time it was dangerous and ridiculous to be a female doctor

After graduation she was denied access to be associated with male doctors. Could not get patients except poor women and children. At first had only 3 patients for a week that she won.

She rented accommodation to practice but other tenant vacated seeing it as a taboo to be a female doctor.

But all these discriminations did not defer Elizabeth. She forced the door open for female doctors. Hurdles and obstacles are meant to be removed, problems to be solved, loads offloaded, dreams realized. Dont let that dream die inside you.

(9) NAME: Apostle Babalola, Joseph Ayodele the precursor of Pentecostalism in Nigeria. His Oke-Oye Revival gave birth to what is now known as Christ Apostolic church (CAC), a Nigerian indigenous church.

BACKGROUND: He studied up to standard Five at All Saints School Oshogbo when he quitted into motor mechanic apprentice. Later he joined public works department (PWD) as steamroller driver.

HIS CALL: His call was specific and a personal call from God. By September 25, 1928, he could not sleep for weeks and had no knowledge of the cause of such strange experiences. While at work his steamroller stopped without a cause and in this dilemma he heard a thundering voice three times saying that if he did not heed the divine call he would die. Like other Bible prophets he avoided this voice. Later he obeyed and resigned his job.

THE CHALLENGE: With little education and heeding Gods call, Babalola became the precursor and pioneer of great healing revival in Nigeria.

-He also founded the now mega church called CAC

-He has his name, named after a great citadel of learning -Joseph Ayo Babalola University even though he never attended one.

You have no excuse not to excel. Limitations have limits and expiring dates. Dont allow them limit or retard your life and potentials. Cash in on this.

In every problem there is a lesson to learn, an asset to acquire, a rest to restore, a bitterness to sweeten, a load to lighten or a price to pay.

9 THE MAKING OF A CHAMPION

(culled from my book, Discovering Yourself)

Champions are made and not born. Champions feat are acquired and not inherited, earned and not transferred, attained to and not deposited.

A courageous man is a champion in the making. Remember that champions became champions because they championed wars, battles, crisis and teams to victory. They can teach you skills and values but no one can teach you courage

THE CHAMPIONS LETTER (Champions stay in the fight - one of the recipients of my monthly blog Bible Faith Nuggets, sent in this letter)

Once, when I was staying at a hotel in Jamaica, I couldnt sleep because I wasnt yet used to the time difference. At about two in the morning, I was up watching a boxing match on television. It was a twelve-round title match, and the boxer from Mexico was pummeling the boxer from the United States. Every time the American boxer moved forward to fight, the other boxer pounded him. The sixth round came and the U.S. boxer was beaten badly, and at the end of the round, he stumbled back into his corner, sat down on the stool, and sagged as if he were a sack of potatoes. Then I saw something happen. In seconds, several men went to work on him. One grabbed a bucket of water and doused him with it. The next grabbed a soaking-wet sponge and squeezed water all over his face, another applied ointment to soothe his wounds. These men were all talking to him at once, and they were rubbing him down as they talked. Even though he was getting trounced, they were telling him, You can do this. You can get back out there. Youre strong! Youre better than he is! One of the men said, Keep your left hook, okay? Keep your left hook. Hes a slow left.

You can get him with that left. After about two minutes, the boxer jumped up, saying, Yeah! Oh, Yeah! He ran back out there, and everything changed in the seventh round. Guess who won the fight? The one who had been about to quit in the sixth round won the fight and received the prize. There was blood everywhere, but under that blood was the champion.

When he won the decision, all his strength came back. He ran around the room screaming. When you win, you forget all the pounding you received during the fight. Sometimes, you may get beaten up pretty badly in life, but stay in the fight.

Fight until you feel the joy of victory. When you think youre going to lose, and you stumble back into the corner of life, the Lord will come and pour the cool water of His Word on your head. He will release the ointment of the Holy Spirit so you can jump back out and say, Hey! Come on, Life! Just like the boxers coaching team, the Holy Spirit speaks good things into your spirit, such as Greater is he that is in you, than he that is in the world. (1 John 4:4 KJV).

Winners earned the process before receiving the accolade. Life will be tough, but get back out there and start throwing blows. Keep your left up and also keep your right hand ready

Life will be tough, but get back out there and start throwing blows. Keep your left up and also keep your right ready. Thats persistence. We know that God wants us to be fighters because the Bible calls us soldiers. (See 2 Timothy 2:3-4). We are warriors. We are people of battle. We dont just receive medals from God. We earn them. If God didnt want you to fight, He would have given you the medal without the conflict. Stay in the fight.

A courageous man is a champion in the making. Remember that champions became champions because they championed wars, battles, crisis and teams to victory. They can teach you skills and values but no one can teach you courage

THE CHAMPIONS REMEMBERING TONIC

Remember to discourage your discouragement and put them where they belong under your feet.

Remember to encourage your courage when you face an uphill task.

Remember to let positive thought and confession swallow up your negative thought and confession when the need arises.

Remember not to complain about the matter but construct, compose, compass and conquer when the matter revolts and bites hard.

Remember who you are by Gods divine plan and strive to fit into his divine pattern.

Remember to rebuke the discouraging and dissenting voices and welcome the positive thinking voice.

Remember to confess what God says you are at all times and in every situation.

Remember you have an adversary in time of adversity that will want you to fail so accordingly address him rightly.

Remember the rules of success and play the game accordingly right.

Remember that one failure is not that you have failed but that you have learned something you didnt do well in your last effort.

Remember that victors are only victims who crossed to the other side. Dont get stocked in front of any obstacle. Jump over.

Remember that warriors are not worry (ers). Worries never solve any problem but warriors do.

Remember that success is failure conversion so create wealth out of all poverty ashes.

Remember that victory only come by fighting and winning wars. Therefore fight and faint not.

Remember that at the end of the tunnel is a huge light and that your sun will shine there and again. So, oil your bearing balls and stay with the Son.

We know that God wants us to be fighters because the Bible called us soldiers .We are warriors. We are people of battle. We dont just receive medals from God. We earn them. If God didnt want you to fight, He would have given you the medal without the conflict. Stay in the fight.

Remember that one failure is not that you have failed but that you have learned something you idnt do well in your last effort

CHAMPIONS ARE MADE

Championships are won. Winners of championships earn it. They showed interest (registered), participated (got involved) and then excelled (won). Winners earned the process before receiving the accolade.

Medals are earned not received. Even honorary degrees, awards, conferment are merited.

Prizes have a price. Prizes are priced and bought. A prize involves a cost or price. Those who pay this price wins and become champions. The reign of a champion depicts a time frame, a rise and a fall. So to remain a champion you have to stay in the race.

THE MAKING OF A CHAMPION

Facing Challenges

Those who never face opposition always stop at proposition. Those who never confront obstacles will always live with postponements and delays. The face of a challenge provokes the sound of battles and competitions. Fighting battles and competing with competitors is the truth and baseline of every challenge.

Trying out something new, something different, something unusual is the creation of facing real challenges. Dealing will obstacles as they come is the sweet of facing challenges. Solving problems is the truth of facing challenges.

The challenge of the champion Goliath became the creator of a double champion in David. The fear and failure of the fall of Sauls challenge became the faith and success of the rise of Davids challenge.

They sang that Saul has killed thousands (quantified success) but David have killed ten thousands (quantified, qualified and certified success).

Sound image creates sound object and verse versa. Begin to deal with your inside so that your outside will present a better deal. Project your inner virtues or values and pronounce your outer qualities. Polish you potential so as to shine your credentials Develop and build a strong and quality concept of yourself

BIG HEART: Awaken the sleeping giant, the champion in you. Champions are people of big heart. The bigness is vis-à-vis the big challenge or task. A mediocre cannot make a master. Pump your heart. The muscles and valves of the heart face the challenges of the blood pressure to keep circulation of food, drugs, and life in the blood to all parts of the living being. Think big, dream big. Well-created ambitions as opposed to inordinate ambitions will keep you on the right track. You are a mirror of the image of yourself or a shadow of the champion in you. Image- making. Tall object begets tall image. Sound object creates sound image. Begin to deal with your inside so that your outside will present a better deal and bargain. Project your inner virtues or values and pronounce your outer qualities. Polish you potential so as to shine your credentials Develop and build a strong and quality concept of yourself and relationship with your community. Bring out the leader in you, and then you will spontaneously generate a great followership on the outside.

The challenge of the champion Goliath became the creator of a double champion in David. The fear and failure of the fall of Sauls challenge became the faith and success of the rise of Davids challenge

FAITH & CONFESSION: Confession they say brings possession but faith ensures and insures completion or perfection. Faith involves body language (the action) and voice language (the words). Champions match words with actions. Champion believes in themselves, their potentials, so they cut it out as they speak it out.

Faith and a corresponding actions, attitude, discipline, training will put you on the pedestal to greatness.

Watch boxers or wrestlers their speeches, behaviors, their muscles, their training, their discipline and even dieting you see a lot of faith and trust that what they do and say will see them to the top. They talk and behave as if they are there already. Faith sends positive signals in the right direction. It takes faith and fight to make a champion.

10 A FINAL WORD

(Culled from my book, Discovering Yourself)

THE POWER OF IDEAS (The Think Tank Power):

Idea is a thought or picture in the mind. It is the seed that produce the giant tree. It is the fetus that developed into a champion man. It is the starter that resulted in the finisher, the root of the Iroko, the architect of the achiever, the genesis of the genius, the alpha of the Omega.

Idea is productive when explored and exploited. Invest in a God-given idea and youll be creating a whole and secured future.

DEALING WITH DISCOURAGEMENT -Discouragement is a tool of delay, a means of frustration and a vehicle of non-fulfillment. Failure is the end of discouragement (In times of Discouragement use these daily encouragement tonic)

-In times of discouragement discourage your discouragement.

-Discourage your fall and encourage your rise.

-Self-encouragement is a strong determinant factor in the face of survival of the fittest or race for survival.

-Show me a discouraged man and I will show you a discarded and rejected success.

-The force that engineers discouragement can be reengineered to propel encouragement.

-Courage is the medicine for opposition.

-Courage is the defeat of failure.

-Courage is the failure of defeat.

-Courage is the failure of failure and the defeat of defeat.

-Courage expressed is a coupling coupon to success and meal ticket.

-A courageous man is a champion in the making.

DEALING WITH OPPORTUNITIES: There are opportunities for goods and services. Opportunities to create wealth, to help someone and be helped back in the process, to showcase your worth or improve your level, to turn your weakness into strength, to correct your mistakes and turn your failure into success. Opportunities are small and big, local and international. The big ones you have been waiting for endlessly might need the small one to activate it. So dont waste time waiting for the big one. Start small with the small ones. Knock at that door even when you dont like the shape and size. Behind it might be the answers you have been waiting for. Make the call. You might hear the voice of opportunity and breakthrough. If you fail, please try again and again until you score the goal. Take that trip; a change of location might be what you need to do the magic or rather the miracle.

SUN Tzu was cited to have said rightly, opportunities multiplies as they are seized

Opportunities abound everywhere and come every day, in different shades and shapes, colors and disposition. Everybody is looking for it but only few see it and grab it. They come in problems (wanting solutions, whether corporate or expert),in disasters (waiting for management expertise),in sickness (seeking medical help or health remedies),in social needs (demanding social crusaders attention),in examination failures (for career counselors, educators intervention, success tip books),in leadership crisis (needing upgrade and update workshops and seminars),in low sales (looking for market strategy tips) or in difficulties (employment opportunities for advisory and consultant personnel).

and consultant personnel).

The story of two visitors to India is an allegory to this truth. While the first was dismayed by the abject poverty all over the place, with bare footed, hungry looking, low esteemed people all around, the second visitor saw an opportunity to make fortune. He built a Shoe Factory that produced millions of shoes which made him rich. What do you see around you? Failure or success, prospect or probability, poverty or prosperity?

I am sure that opportunities properly accessed and harnessed have prospects and can create wealth but what am not sure of is how productive is procrastination, undue waiting, ungodly delays, worrying or prolonged trying-to-figure-it-out.

I am sure that opportunities properly accessed and harnessed have prospects and can create wealth but what I am not sure of is how productive is procrastination, undue waiting, ungodly delays, worrying or prolonged trying-to-figure-it-out.

See opportunity, grab opportunity, act on and respond to opportunity, adjust and realign and it will amaze you what you have been missing. Looking for a job? Write out the problems of the locality or government or schools or women, men, children, house pets or health problems and develop solutions for your potential recipients for a little charge and you are there, a job and wealth creator and no longer a job seeker.

WHAT? -THE WHAT QUESTIONS AND ANSWERS. The patterns that make you what you worth the man you are today and will be tomorrow.

What do you have? - Possession

What do you see? Vision

What do you think? Creative thought pattern or Imagination. Inventive and synthetic build-ups.

What do you do? Actions/Activity.

What do you do with what you see, what you do, what you think and what you have? A mans gift (possession), will make way for him. In the original language, gift is also rendered as giving or offering. So a Mans giving or offerings (i.e. what you have in you that you release, not just what is innate and dormant in you. It is the talents or gifts that you have that you make available, release or manifest that will announce you and not the ones in you unavailable, unreleased and unprocessed). If nobody knows about or sees your talent, of what use is it to you or anyone. Procure it, process it, produce it and it will paint a portrait of the gem you are inside and outside. What you have may be knowledge, talent, wisdom, money, education, associates, or contacts. What you have can be conceptual, contextual or content

Self-encouragement is a strong determinant factor in the face of survival of the fittest or race for survival. -Show me a discouraged man and I will show you a discarded and rejected success

Who are you? What potential deposits are you carrying? What purpose, assignment, calling, destiny, were you created to fulfill. You must discover who you are and do something about it.

APPRECIATION

Thanks for finding time to read this. I hope you have been blessed. I will appreciate if you share this with your friends and write a customer review and rating down the book page online as it will help others share from this blessing too. Thanks so much and may God's divine favor follow you. God bless you and thanks for visiting. Expect more and bigger blessings.

APPENDIX A: ACHIEVERS BEST GUIDE SERIES (ACHIEVERS HANDBOOKS 1- 5)

*****

*****

THE MAKING OF HIGH ACHIEVERS

- Check out Achievers handbook, books 1 - 5 online for more. Each handbook contains over 100 Achievers nuggets and inspirational" keys that will help you fulfill your destiny. Bon Voyage!

ABOUT THE AUTHOR

Pastor Ikechukwu Joseph, the author of "Discovering Yourself" is a notable song writer, poet, author and the publisher of bestselling "Unlocking Closed Doors, Strategic Spiritual Warfare, Haunting Shadows, Studies in the Book of Colossians (a verse by verse analytical study commentary), Studies in the Book of Philippians (a verse by verse analytical study commentary) and Angels Go to War. He trained as a Science Educator, Biologist, System Engineer and Website Developer. He is a graduate of University of Ibadan (M. Ed), University of Port Harcourt (B. SC) and a duly accredited ordained Minister with Evangelistic Messengers Association International, Tennessee, U.S.A. Pastor Joseph served God under different organizations like The Scripture Union, Four Square Gospel Church, NIFES, Fellowship of Christian Students, Grace of God Mission, and Believers Gospel Mission before God led him into the Harvest field.

AUTHOR'S CONTACT

Email:
tlwgom@yahoo.com
Telephone:
+2348035033228
+2348022957255
###
Connect with Me Online
Sign up for our newsletter: http://eepurl.com/b_ouQn
Twitter: http://twitter.com/ikechukwujosep1
Facebook: http://facebook.com/ikechukwu2joseph
Wattpad: http://wattpad.com/ikechukwu2joseph

www.ingramcontent.com/pod-product-compliance
Lightning Source LLC
Chambersburg PA
CBHW030039230526
45472CB00002B/593